# THE STUFF STARS ARE MADE OF

Written by
## Dr. Adam Tuff

Illustrated by
## Kieran Gates

Special Thanks to Dr. Christian Diget & Katherine Leech

from the University of York's Binding Blocks

Nuclear Physics outreach project

Do you know what the Sun is?

The Sun shines down upon the Earth
and brings the light of day,
its heat can melt our ice creams
but it keeps the cold at bay.

Our bodies breathe in oxygen
which we get from the air,
made with light by means with which
our trees and plants take care.

Do you know what stars are,
who at night come out to play?
Stars are like our Sun
but are very far away.

Stars are different sizes
and in colours they're aglow,
here's a story about a star
from a long, long time ago.

Once upon a time
in the emptiness of space,
a big cloud called a nebula
sat in a cold dark place.

In the nebula lived protons
which are very small in size,
in fact they are so tiny
you can't see them with your eyes.

Protons are a part
of the particle family tree,

there are many others like them,
and the neutrons we'll soon see.

Protons liked to move fast,
through the nebula they flew,
soon lots more protons would join in
and whizzed round faster too.

One day there were so many
they collided with a crash,
they bumped and bumped and heated up
and faster they would dash!

When countless protons moved there
the temperature would climb,

it got so hot a star was born...

...and more stars grew in time.

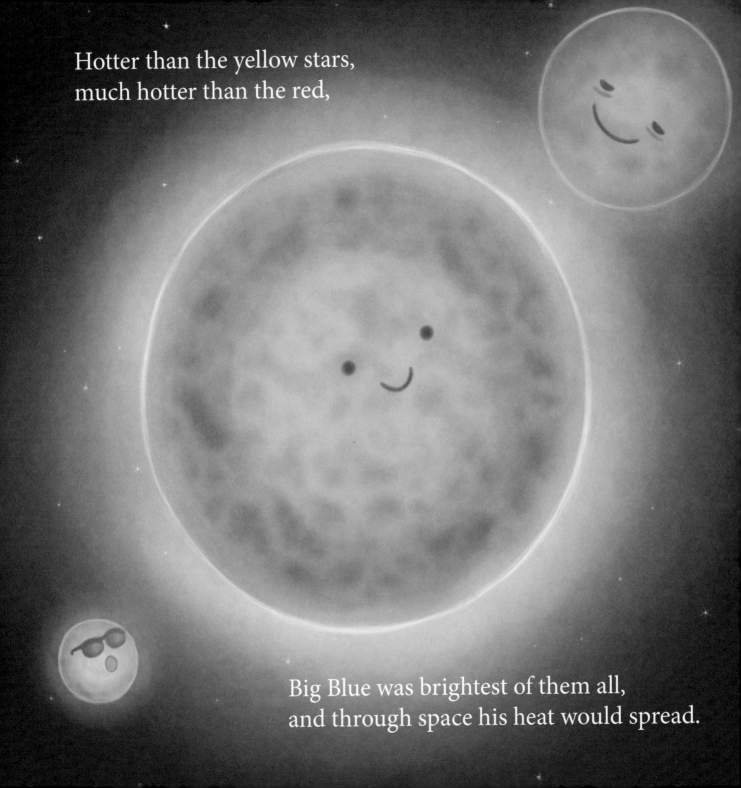

Hotter than the yellow stars,
much hotter than the red,

Big Blue was brightest of them all,
and through space his heat would spread.

It got so hot in Big Blue's tum that protons fused as one,

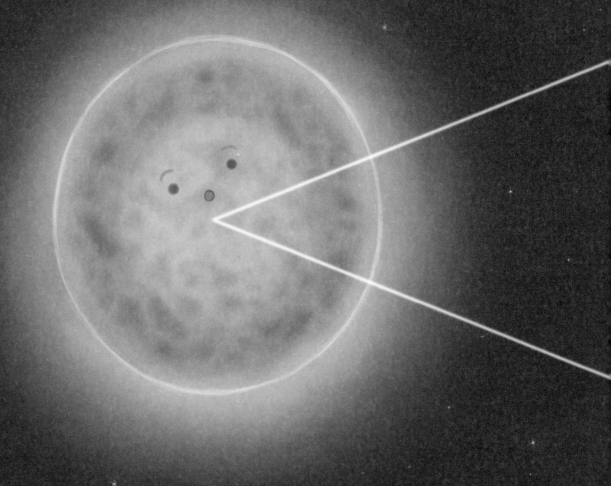

when two protons would fuse and join one changed to a neutron.

The fusing of the protons made lots of heat and light,

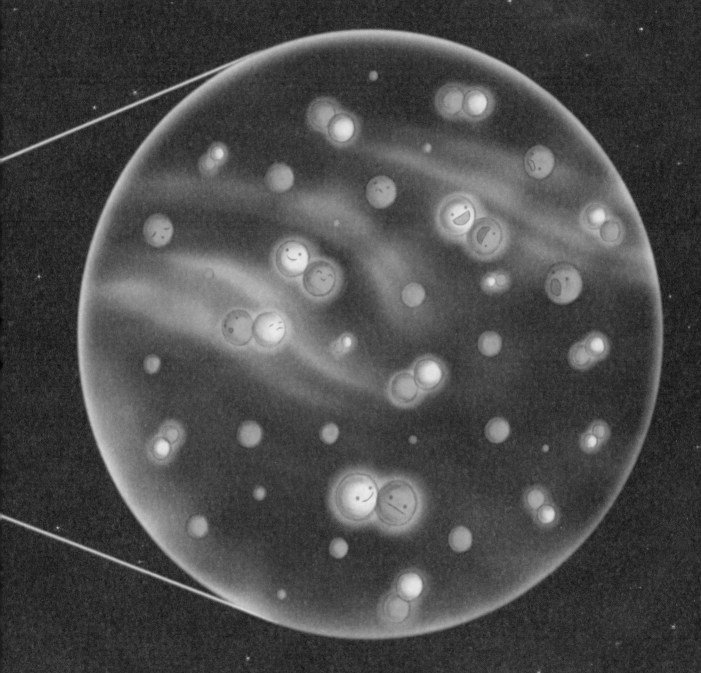

and Big Blue shone so brilliant, the brightest of the bright.

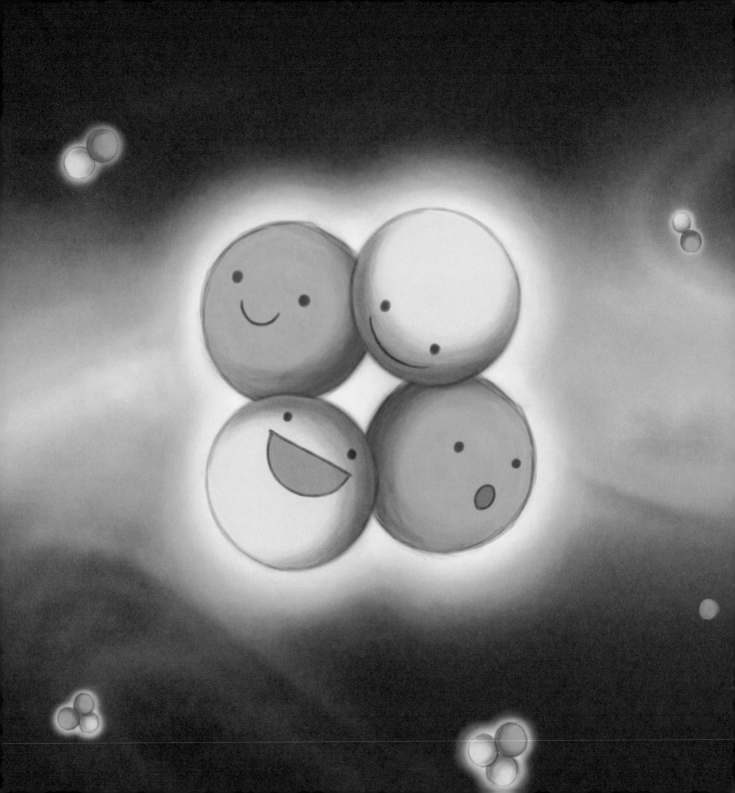

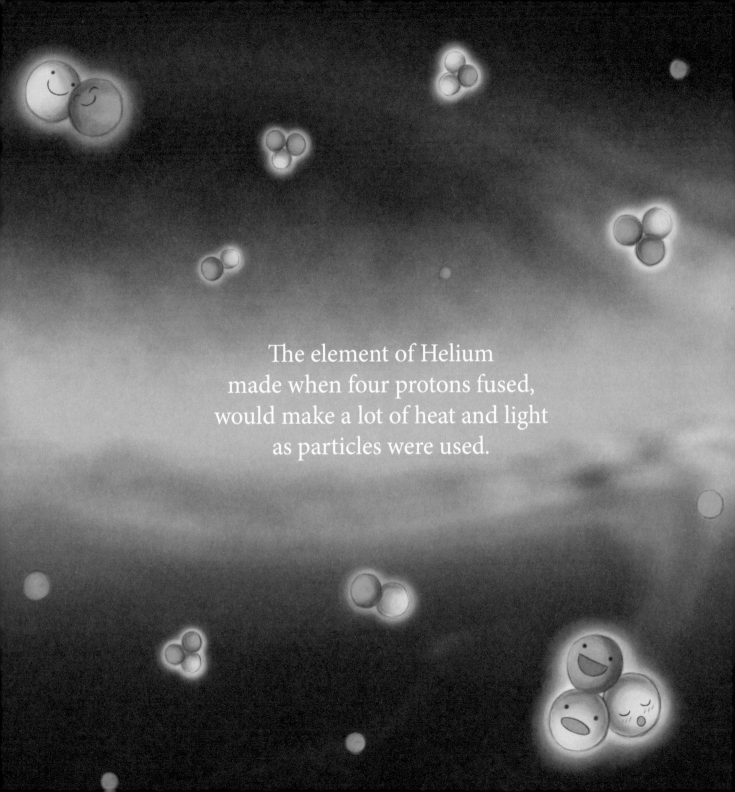

The element of Helium
made when four protons fused,
would make a lot of heat and light
as particles were used.

The fusing of more protons made lots more heat and light,

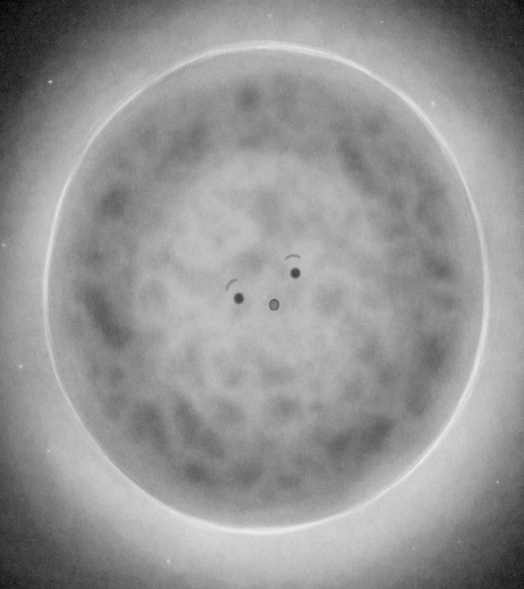

and Big Blue shone more brilliant, the brightest of the bright.

When all protons in Blue's tum fused and Helium could not,

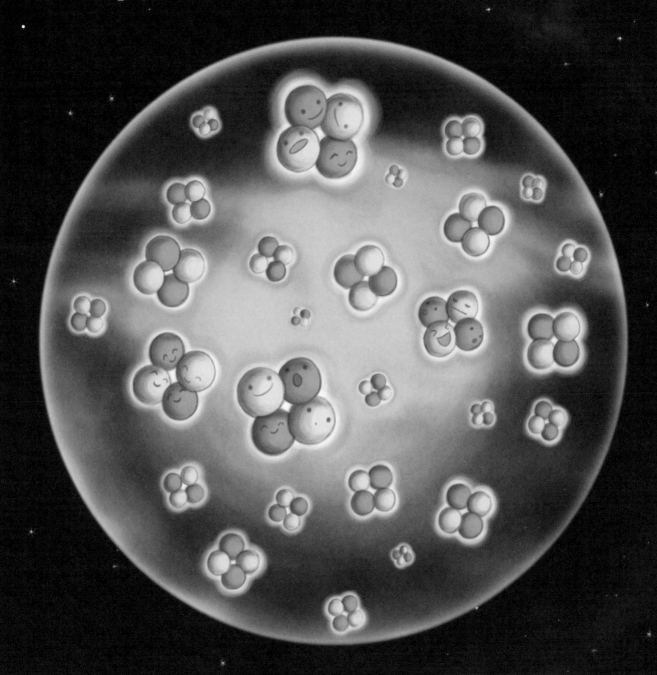

he had to make more heat and light so his tum got very hot.

It got so hot the Helium made elements of great size,

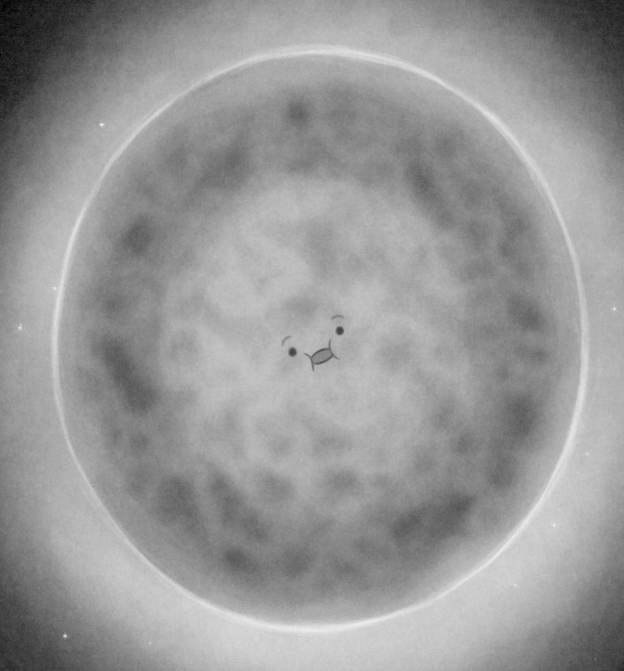

and with new fusing elements, his temperature would rise.

The fusing of big elements made lots of heat and light,

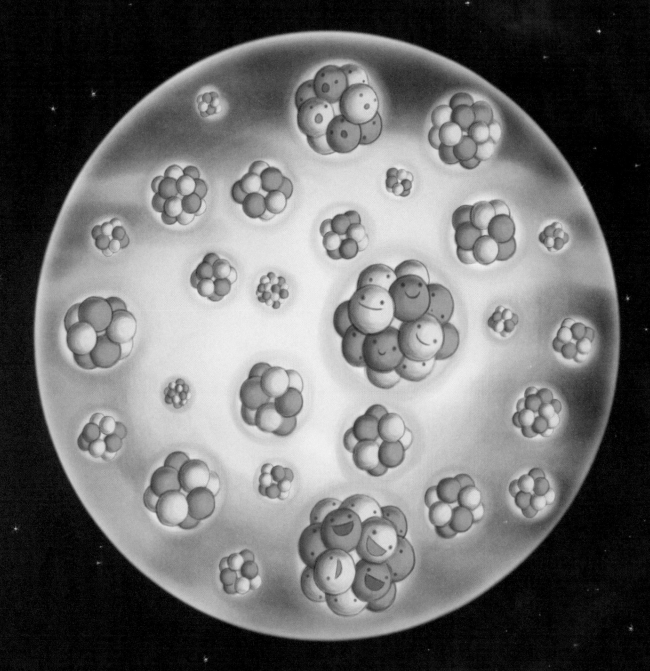

and soon Blue's tummy got so full, but still he shone most bright.

Big Blue had got so huge he burst - his tum filled to the brim,

the bang made so much starlight, that the other stars looked dim.

Poor Big Blue was now no more, he'd gone without a trace,

His particles and elements flung far off into space.

The elements and particles
with nowhere left to go,
made new homes in outer space
and over time they'd grow.

The protons made a nebula
a new star formed within,
the elements made planets
and around the star they'd spin.

They made the moon and all worlds
like Jupiter and Mars,
they even made the Earth and us…

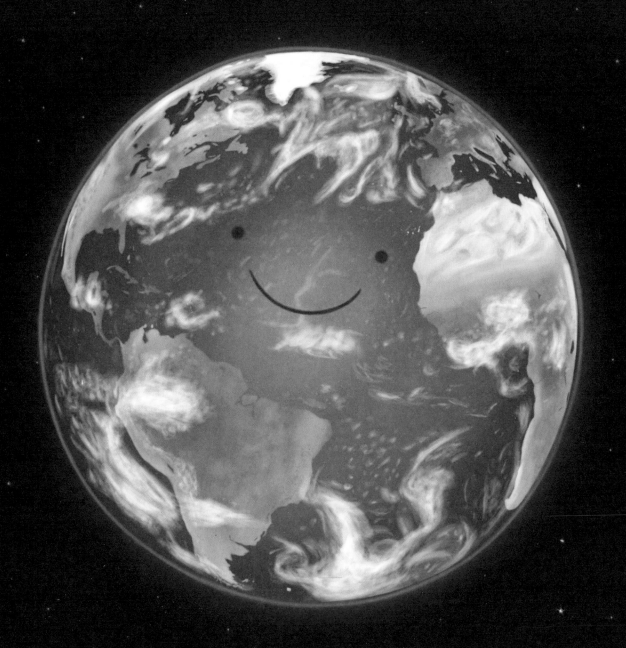

...we are all made of stars!